volume twelve of
the illustrated history of movies through posters

Images from the Hershenson-Allen Archive

Previous Volumes:
Volume One: Cartoon Movie Posters
Volume Two: Cowboy Movie Posters
Volume Three: Academy Award Winners' Movie Posters
Volume Four: Sports Movie Posters
Volume Five: Crime Movie Posters
Volume Six: More Cowboy Movie Posters
Volume Seven: Horror Movie Posters
Volume Eight: Best Pictures' Movie Posters
Volume Nine: Musical Movie Posters
Volume Ten: Serial Movie Posters
Volume Eleven: Horror, Sci-Fi & Fantasy Movie Posters

Edited by Richard Allen and Bruce Hershenson
Published by Bruce Hershenson
P.O. Box 874, West Plains, MO 65775
Phone: (417) 256-9616 Fax: (417) 257-6948
mail@brucehershenson.com (e-mail)
http://www.brucehershenson.com or
http://www.emovieposter.com (website)

INTRODUCTION

Welcome to the twelfth volume of the Illustrated History of Movies Through Posters. While the subject of this book, comedy movies, is one of the most popular genres of film, it is difficult to describe exactly what constitutes a comedy. Most films have at least some comedic elements, but how much comedic content does a film need before it is officially a "comedy"? Since there are no clear-cut rules, I based this book on a few simple guidelines. First, I excluded movies which, although they contain some or many funny scenes, most filmgoers would never classify as a comedy, because they much better fit into some other genre (films such as **Singin' in the Rain** or **Fargo**). Second, I did not include all that many posters from classic comedies of the 1910s to 1930s, as those have been so extensively covered in my auction volumes (all still in print as of this writing). Finally, since this is a book of images, I tried to always give preference to posters that have the most visual appeal, although I have tried to include images from all the most-loved comedies.

However, on occasion I broke my own rules. In this series, I try to present a balance of films from all the years films have been made, so in years in which few comedy films were made, I sometimes had to include lesser choices, and in other years that were strong for comedies I had to exclude some worthwhile posters in order to achieve the balance I aim for. Note that in this book there are far more films from before 1943 and after 1967 than from the period in between. Perhaps as the horrors of World War II became known, filmmakers felt uneasy trying to make feature length comedies, and then in the 1950s and 1960s TV became the primary source of comedy material. Filmmakers sought to counteract this by making "adult" sex comedies in the 1950s and 1960s, but time has not been kind to most of these films, and few are included in this volume.

There are many types of comedies, from the broad slapstick of Jerry Lewis, Mel Brooks and Jim Carrey, to musical comedies such as **The Court Jester** or **Gentlemen Prefer Blondes**, to the great screwball comedies of the 1930s such as **Twentieth Century**, to romantic comedies such as **Love Me Tonight**, to crime comedies such as **A Shot in the Dark** and **Trouble in Paradise**, and on and on. I have tried to cover all of these types of comedies somewhat equally, as there is no saying that one type is more appropriate for this volume than another!

Unless otherwise noted, the image in this volume is of the original U.S. one-sheet poster (the standard movie poster size, measuring 27"x 41"), from the first release of the film. Other sizes included are lobby cards (11"x 14"), window cards (14"x 22"), inserts (14"x 36"), half-sheets (22"x 28"), three-sheets (41"x 81"), six-sheets (81"x 81"), and foreign posters (varying sizes).

All the images in this book come from the Hershenson-Allen Archive. The archive consists of over 35,000 different movie poster images, all photographed directly from the original posters onto high quality 4"x 5"color transparencies. There is not another resource like it anywhere, and it is the world's foremost source of movie poster images. The Archive has provided images for books, videos, DVDs, magazines, and newspapers.

This is not a catalog of posters for sale, nor do I sell any sort of movie poster reproductions! However, I do sell movie posters of all sorts through public auctions, both"ìlive"and over the Internet. If you are interested in acquiring original vintage movie posters (or any of the other books I have published) visit my website at http://www.brucehershenson.com (the most visited vintage movie poster site on the Internet) or send me a self-addressed stamped envelope for free brochures.

I wish to thank Ira Resnick, longtime movie poster collector and owner of the MPA Gallery in New York City (managed by equally longtime collector Joe Burtis). Ira was kind enough to share two extremely rare lobby cards from his collection. I heartily recommend the MPA Gallery to anyone looking to acquire movie poster rarities! I also wish to thank longtime collector Jon Schwartz, who lent me his poster of The Court Jester. It is my personal favorite comedy film of all time, and I could not have let this volume be published without including it.

I need to thank Amy Knight who did the layouts and designed the covers for this book, and Sylvia Hershenson, who assisted in its preparation and did the proofreading. Most of all, I need to thank my partner, Richard Allen. He has always loved movie posters of all years and genres, and he tracked down many of the images in this book. We share a common vision, and we hope to keep publishing these volumes until we have covered every possible genre of film.

I dedicate this book to my longtime friend, Mike Lacey. This is especially fitting, as Mike is the owner of the **Comedy and Magic Club** in Hermosa Beach, California, one of the oldest and best of all the improvisational comedy clubs. Mike has not only been a great friend to me for many years, but he is also one of the finest human beings I have ever met! If you are ever in the Los Angeles area, I urge you to stop in at the **Comedy and Magic Club**. I am sure you'll be glad you did.

Bruce Hershenson
August 2000

1. TILLIE'S PUNCTURED ROMANCE, 1914, special window card

2. THE KID, 1921

3. THE TRAMP, 1915, three-sheet

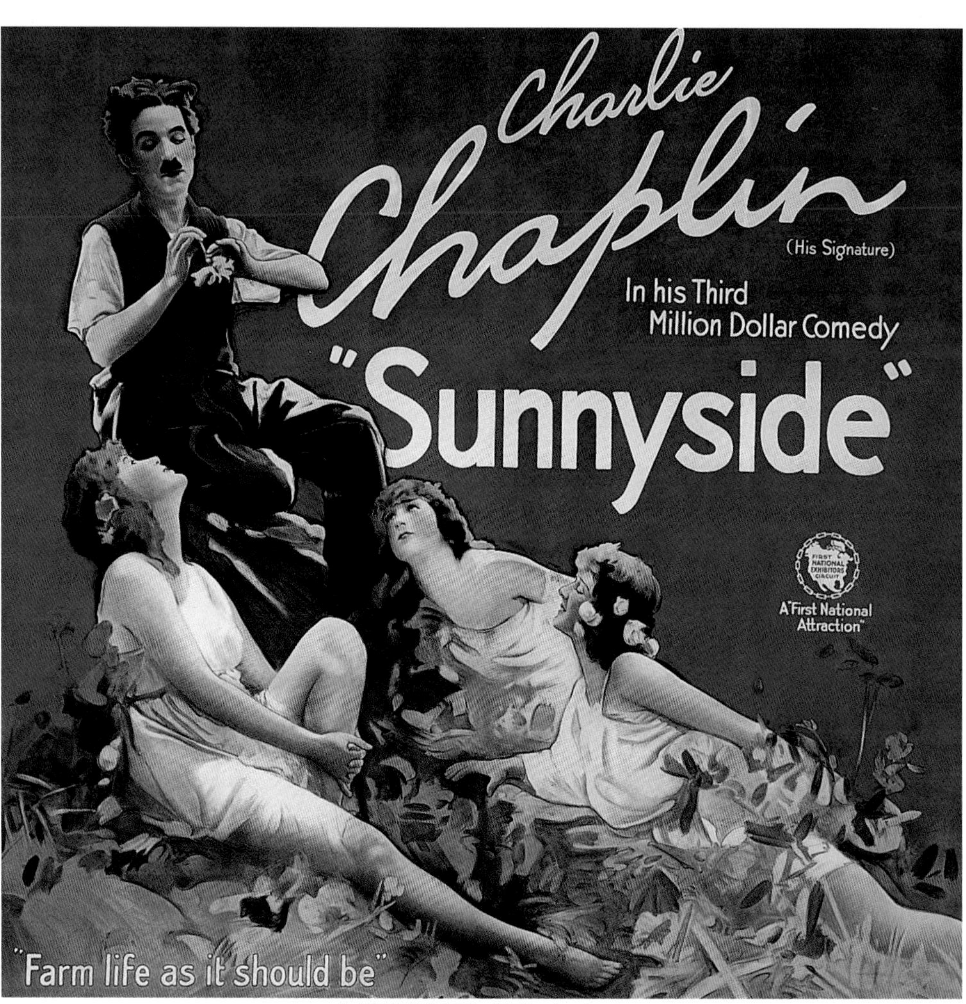

4. SUNNYSIDE, 1919, six-sheet

5. THE GOAT, 1921

6. LOVE AND DOUGHNUTS, 1921

7. DR. JACK, 1922

8. OUR GANG, 1922

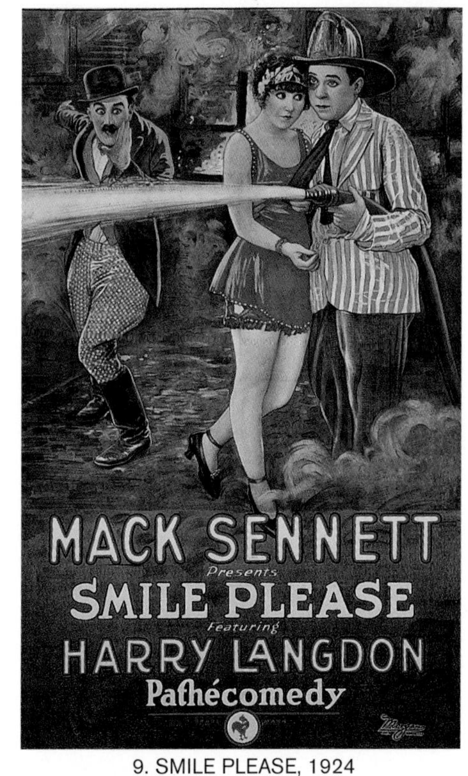

9. SMILE PLEASE, 1924

10. RAGGEDY ROSE, 1926

11. MIGHTY LIKE A MOOSE, 1926

12. THE COHENS & KELLYS, 1926

13. WIFE TAMERS, 1926

14. ALONG CAME AUNTIE, 1926

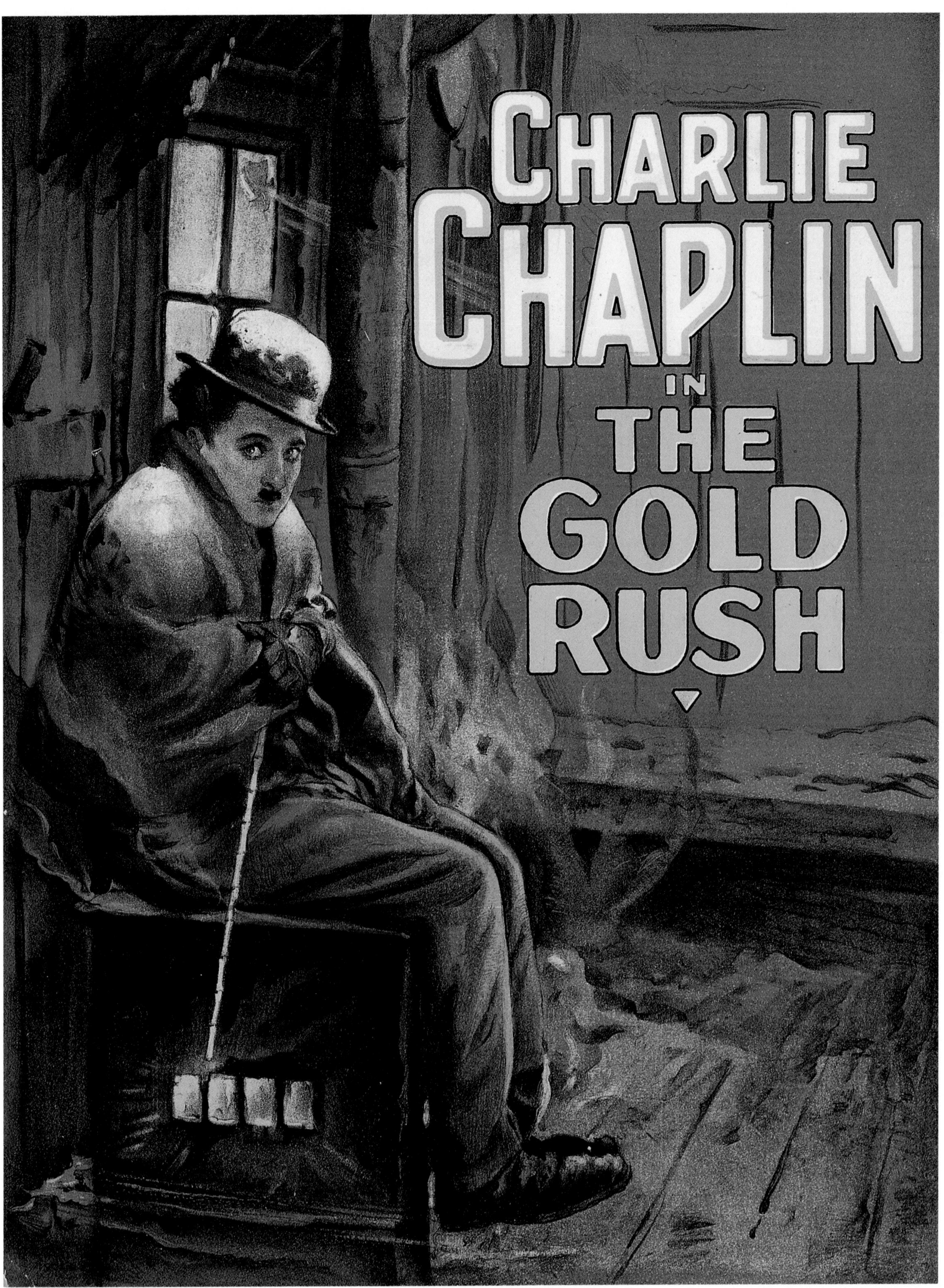

15. THE GOLD RUSH, 1925, window card

16. THE GENERAL, 1927, half-sheet

17. A KISS IN A TAXI, 1927

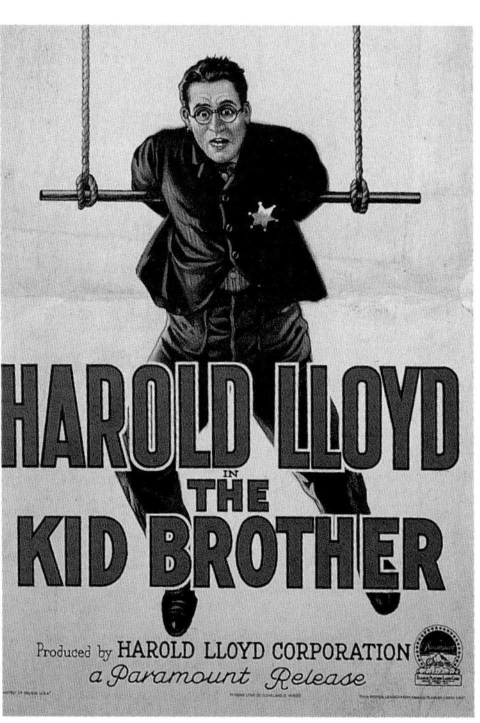

18. THE KID BROTHER, 1927, window card

19. HER WILD OAT, 1927

20. COLLEGE, 1927

21. SAILORS, BEWARE!, 1927

22. THE CAMERAMAN, 1928

23. CLANCY'S KOSHER WEDDING, 1927

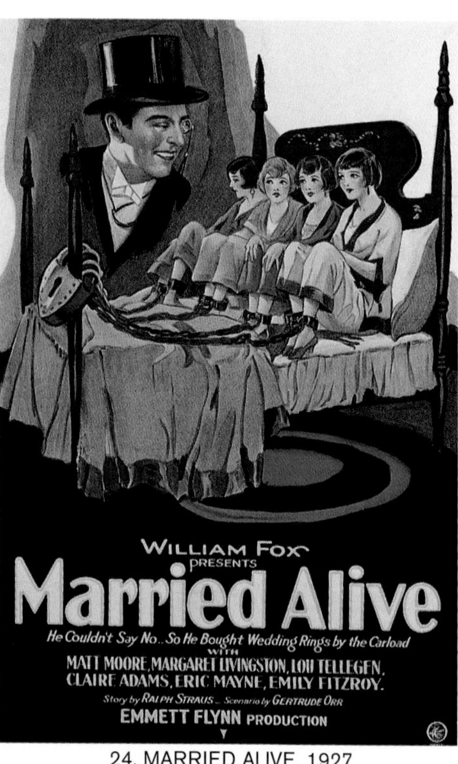

24. MARRIED ALIVE, 1927

25. SPEEDY, 1928

26. LIBERTY, 1929

27. RUNNIN' THRU THE RYE, 1929

28. THE SHANNONS OF BROADWAY, 1929

The MARX BROTHERS
with OSCAR SHAW and MARY EATON
IN
THE COCOANUTS
MUSIC AND LYRICS BY IRVING BERLIN
BOOK BY GEORGE S. KAUFMAN
DIRECTED BY JOSEPH SANTLEY AND ROBERT FLOREY

29. THE COCOANUTS, 1929, insert

30. CHECK AND DOUBLE CHECK, 1930

31. SEA LEGS, 1930

32. SKIRT SHY, 1930

33. ANOTHER FINE MESS, 1930

34. TRUE TO THE NAVY, 1930, lobby card

35. ANIMAL CRACKERS, 1930, lobby card

36. MONKEY BUSINESS, 1931, lobby card

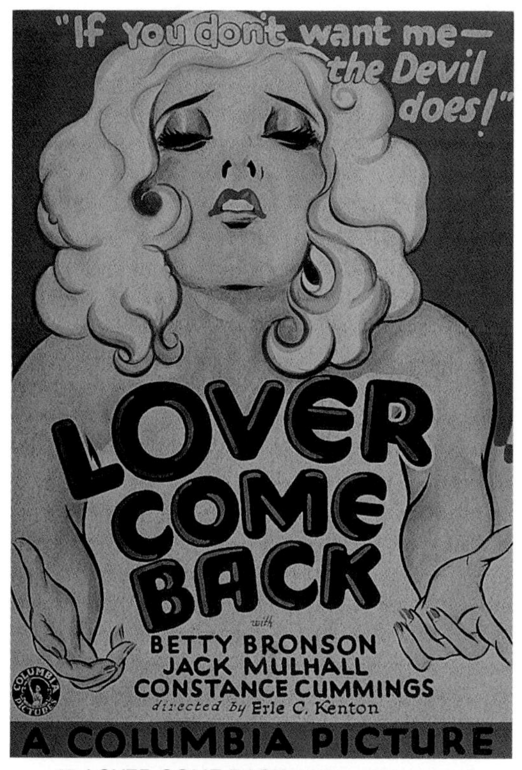

37. LOVER COME BACK, 1931, window card

38. MICKEY'S STAMPEDE, 1931

39. CITY LIGHTS, 1931, three-sheet

40. BEAU HUNKS, 1931

41. SIDEWALKS OF NEW YORK, 1931

42. LAUGH AND GET RICH, 1931

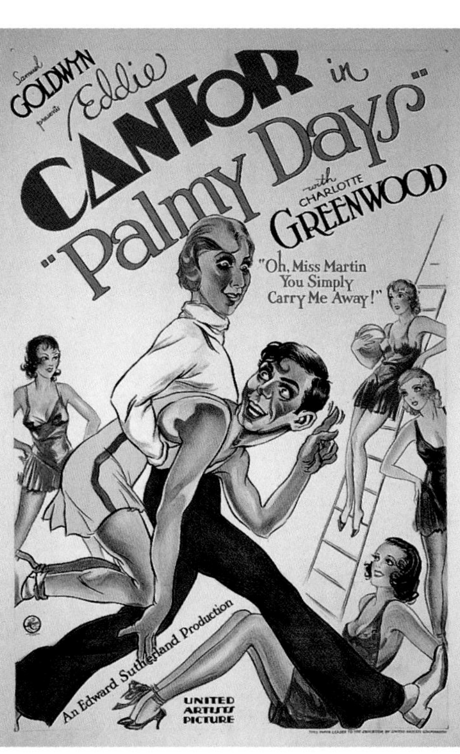

43. PALMY DAYS, 1931

44. CAUGHT PLASTERED, 1931

45. THE MUSIC BOX, 1932, lobby card

46. MILLION DOLLAR LEGS, 1932

47. GIRL CRAZY, 1932

48. HORSE FEATHERS, 1932

49. PACK UP YOUR TROUBLES, 1932

50. JEWEL ROBBERY, 1932

51. ONE HOUR WITH YOU, 1932

52. AN OLD SPANISH CUSTOM, 1932

53. MOVIE CRAZY, 1932

54. LOVE ME TONIGHT, 1932, lobby card

55. TROUBLE IN PARADISE, 1932, lobby card

56. DINNER AT EIGHT, 1933

57. THE KID FROM BORNEO, 1933

58. THE DEVIL'S BROTHER, 1933

59. ROMAN SCANDALS, 1933

60. LADY FOR A DAY, 1933

61. SONS OF THE DESERT, 1933, window card

62. SHE DONE HIM WRONG, 1933, threesheet

63. TILLIE AND GUS, 1933, window card

64. DUCK SOUP, 1933

65. STATE FAIR, 1933

66. ELMER, THE GREAT, 1933

67. 20TH CENTURY, 1934, half sheet

68. SMARTY, 1934

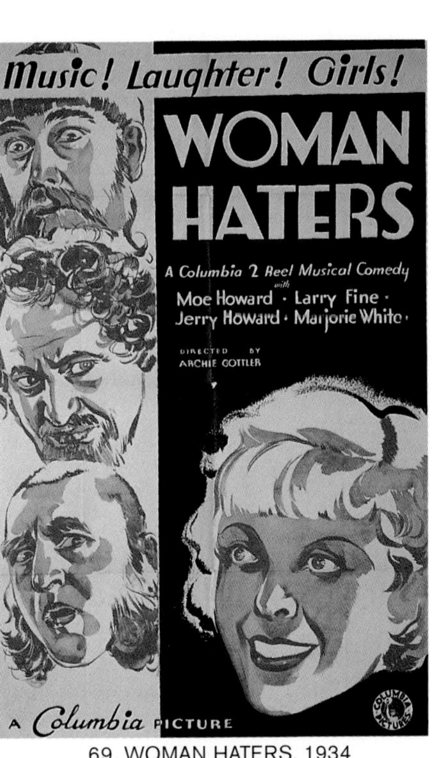

69. WOMAN HATERS, 1934

70. JIMMY THE GENT, 1934

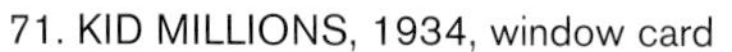
71. KID MILLIONS, 1934, window card

72. KENTUCKY KERNELS, 1934, three-sheet

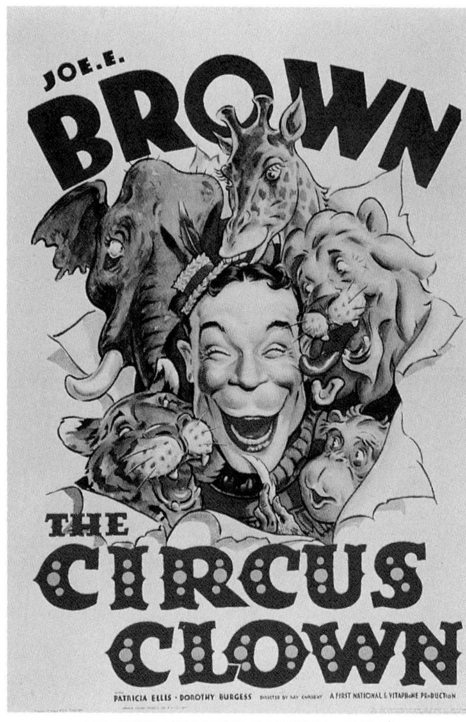

73. THE CIRCUS CLOWN, 1934

74. MRS. WIGGS OF THE CABBAGE PATCH, 1934

75. STRICTLY DYNAMITE, 1934

76. IT'S A GIFT, 1934

77. A NIGHT AT THE OPERA, 1935, lobby card

78. MAN ON THE FLYING TRAPEZE, 1935

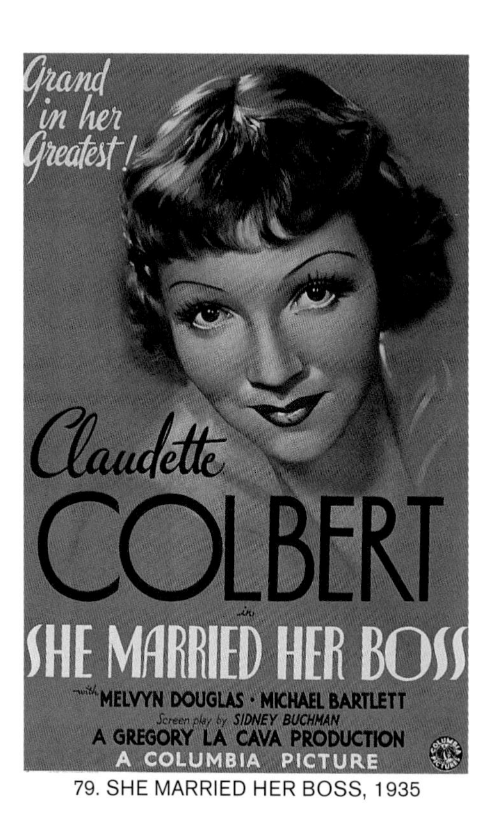

79. SHE MARRIED HER BOSS, 1935

80. DON'T BET ON BLONDES, 1935

81. MY MAN GODFREY, 1936, window card

82. MR. DEEDS GOES TO TOWN, 1936

83. SUZY, 1936, window card

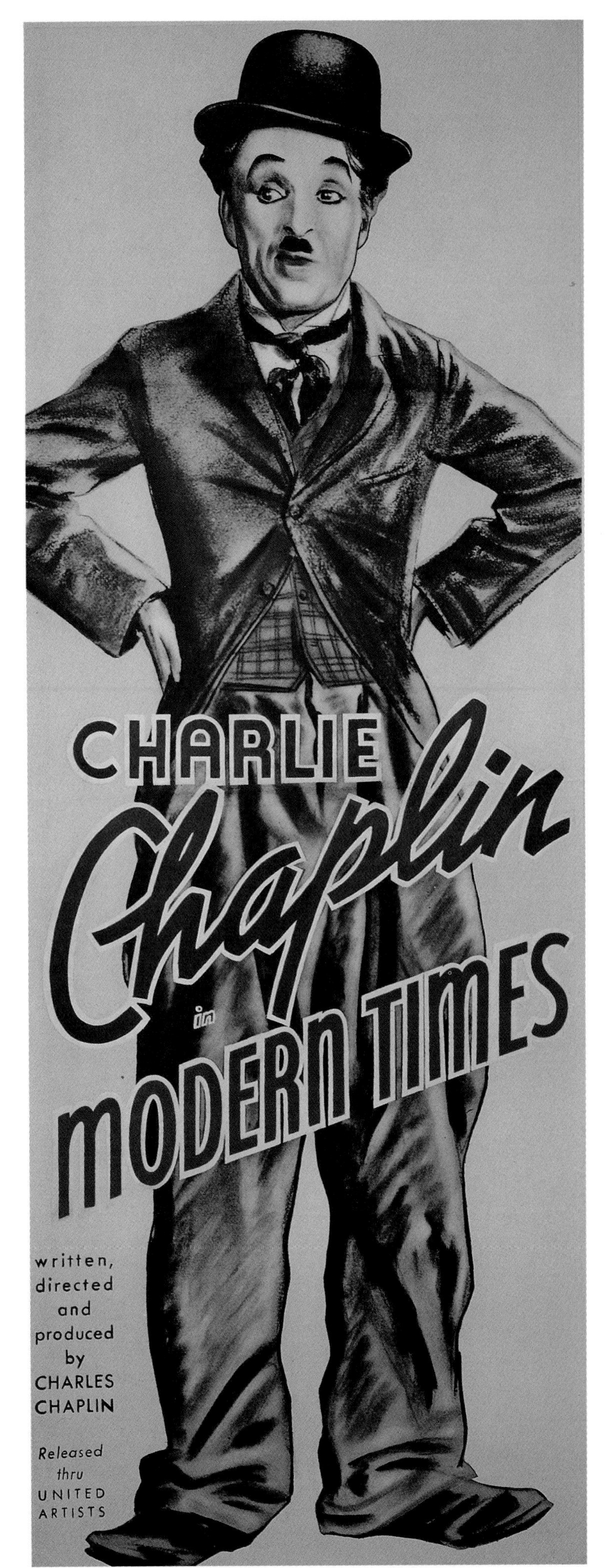

84. MODERN TIMES, 1936, insert

85. LIBELED LADY, 1936

86. SMARTEST GIRL IN TOWN, 1936

87. OUR RELATIONS, 1936

88. LOVE BEFORE BREAKFAST, 1936

89. POPPY, 1936

90. THE AWFUL TRUTH, 1937

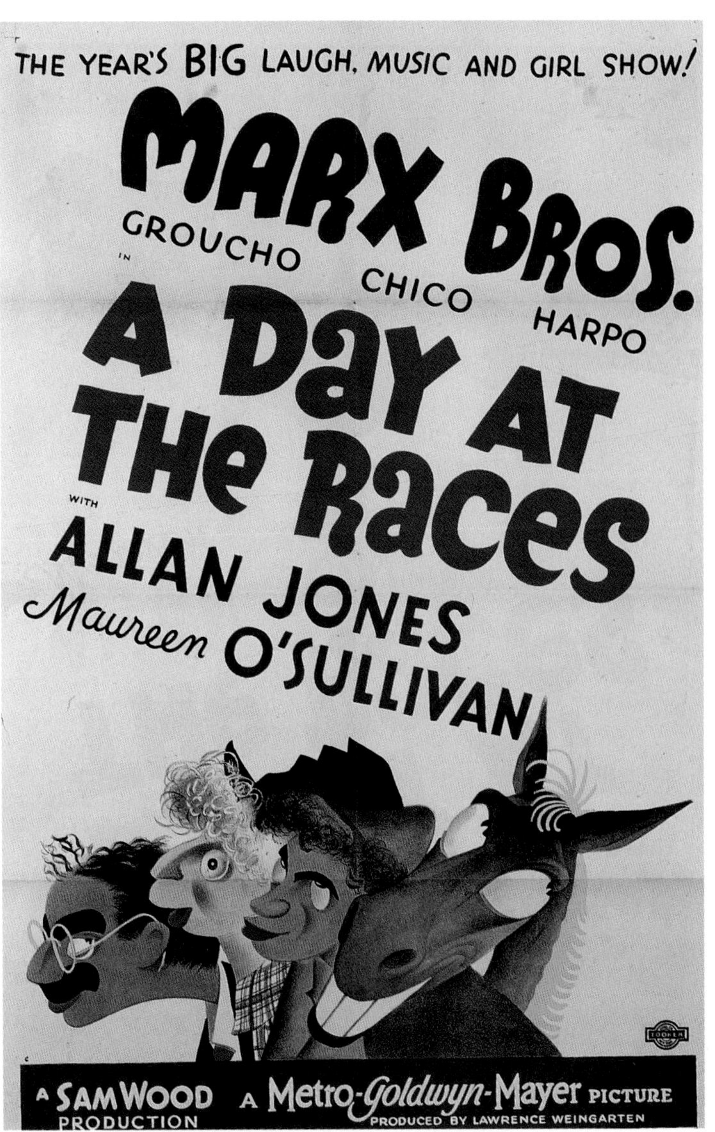

91. A DAY AT THE RACES, 1937

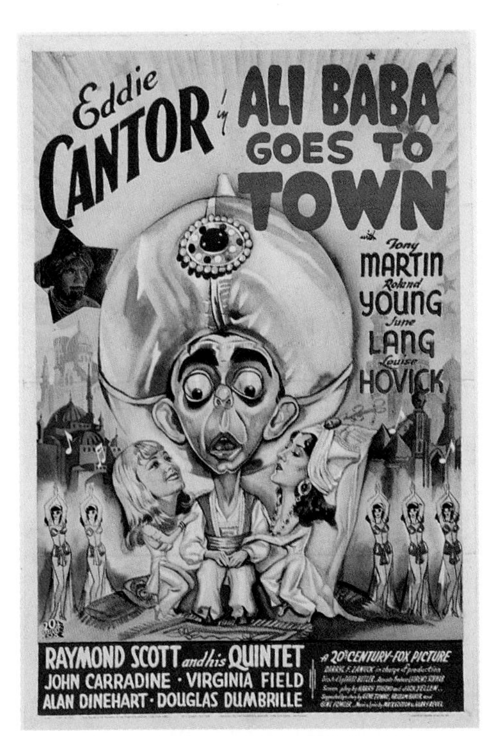

92. ALI BABA GOES TO TOWN, 1937

93. TOPPER, 1937

94. THE PERFECT SPECIMEN, 1937

95. BRINGING UP BABY, 1938, title card

96. BLUEBEARD'S 8TH WIFE, 1938

97. BLOCK-HEADS, 1938

98. VIVACIOUS LADY, 1938

99. BLONDIE, 1938

100. $1,000 A TOUCHDOWN, 1939

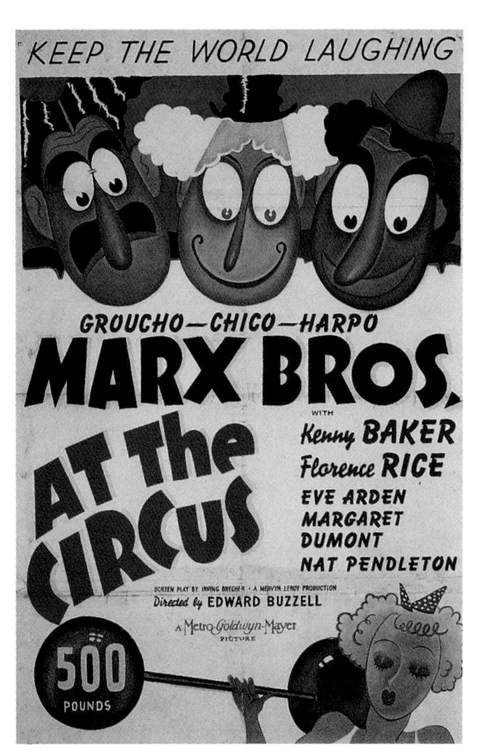

101. AT THE CIRCUS, 1939

102. MAISIE, 1939

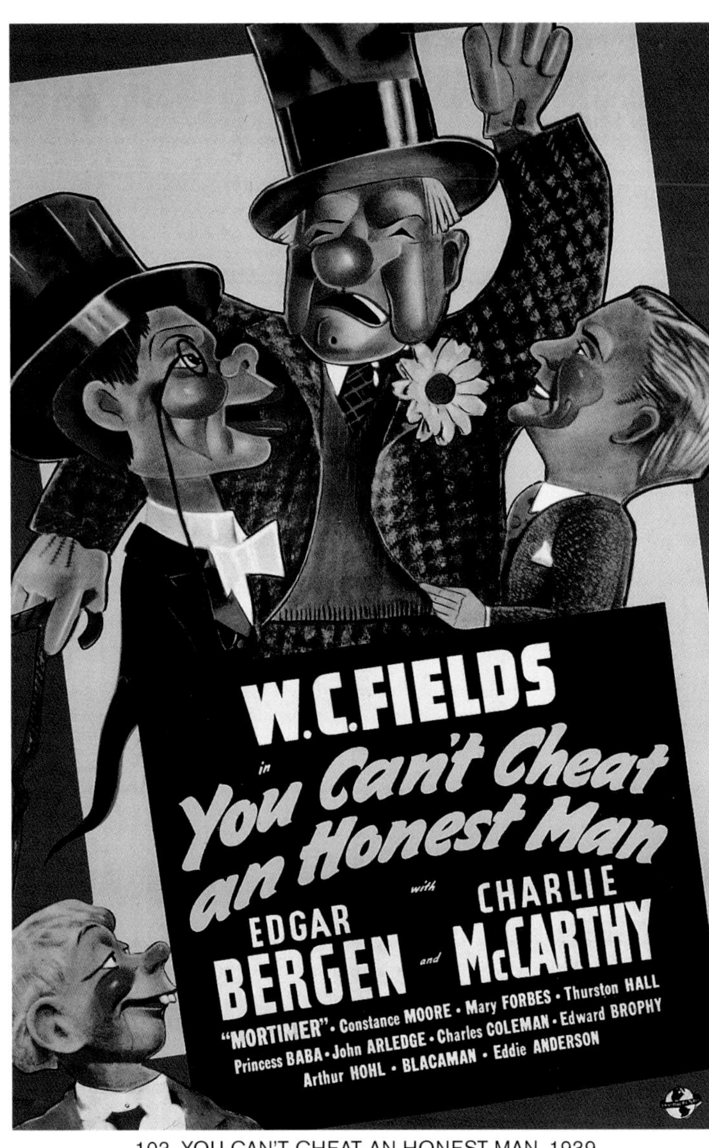

103. YOU CAN'T CHEAT AN HONEST MAN, 1939

104. CHARLIE MCCARTHY, DETECTIVE, 1939

105. SAPS AT SEA, 1940, title card

106. LI'L ABNER, 1940, title card

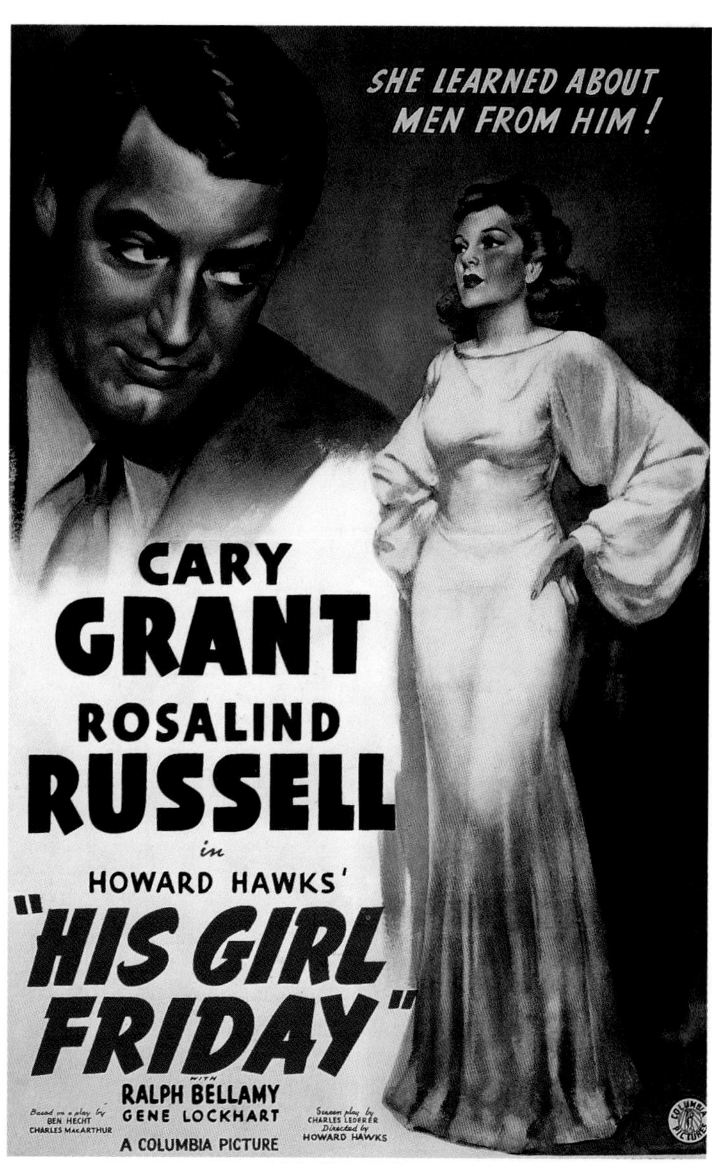

107. HIS GIRL FRIDAY, 1940

108. LOVE THY NEIGHBOR, 1940

109. BROTHER ORCHID, 1940

110. MY FAVORITE WIFE, 1940

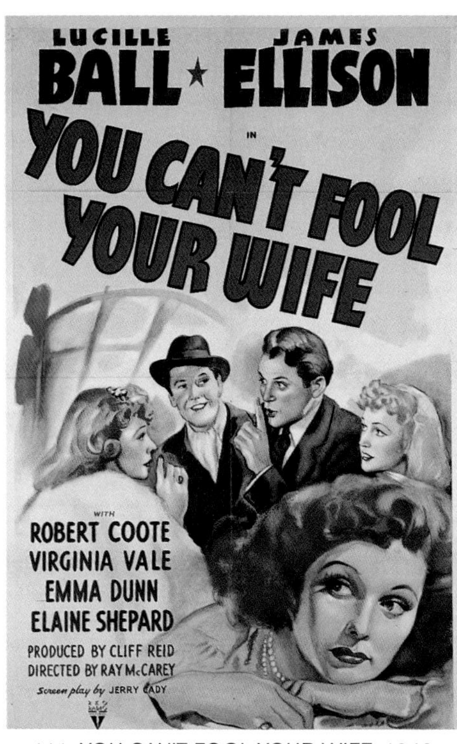

111. YOU CAN'T FOOL YOUR WIFE, 1940

112. ROAD TO SINGAPORE, 1940

113. REMEMBER THE NIGHT, 1940

114. MY LITTLE CHICKADEE, 1940

115. THE SHOP AROUND THE CORNER, 1940

116. ROAD TO ZANZIBAR, 1941

117. THE LADY EVE, 1941

118. LOOK WHO'S LAUGHING, 1941

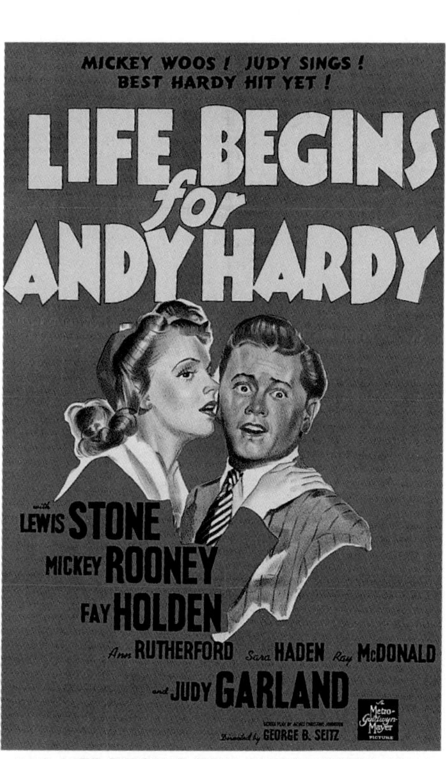

119. LIFE BEGINS FOR ANDY HARDY, 1941

120. NEVER GIVE A SUCKER AN EVEN BREAK, 1941

121. THE PALM BEACH STORY, 1942

122. ROAD TO MOROCCO, 1942

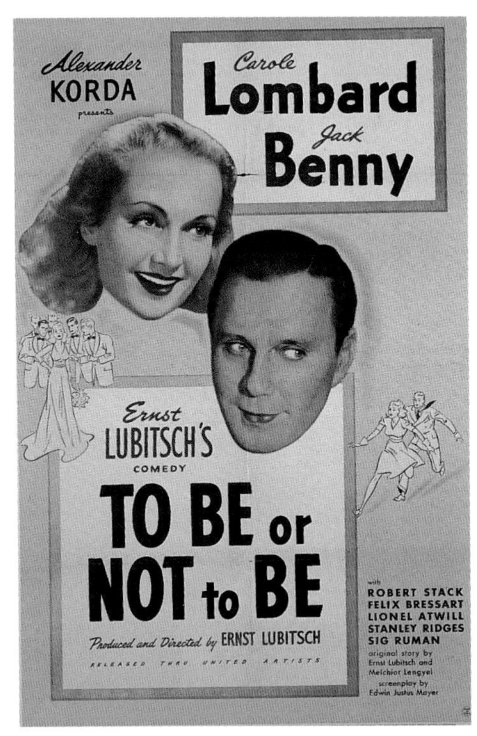

123. TO BE OR NOT TO BE, 1942

124. HERE WE GO AGAIN, 1942

125. THE MAJOR AND THE MINOR, 1942

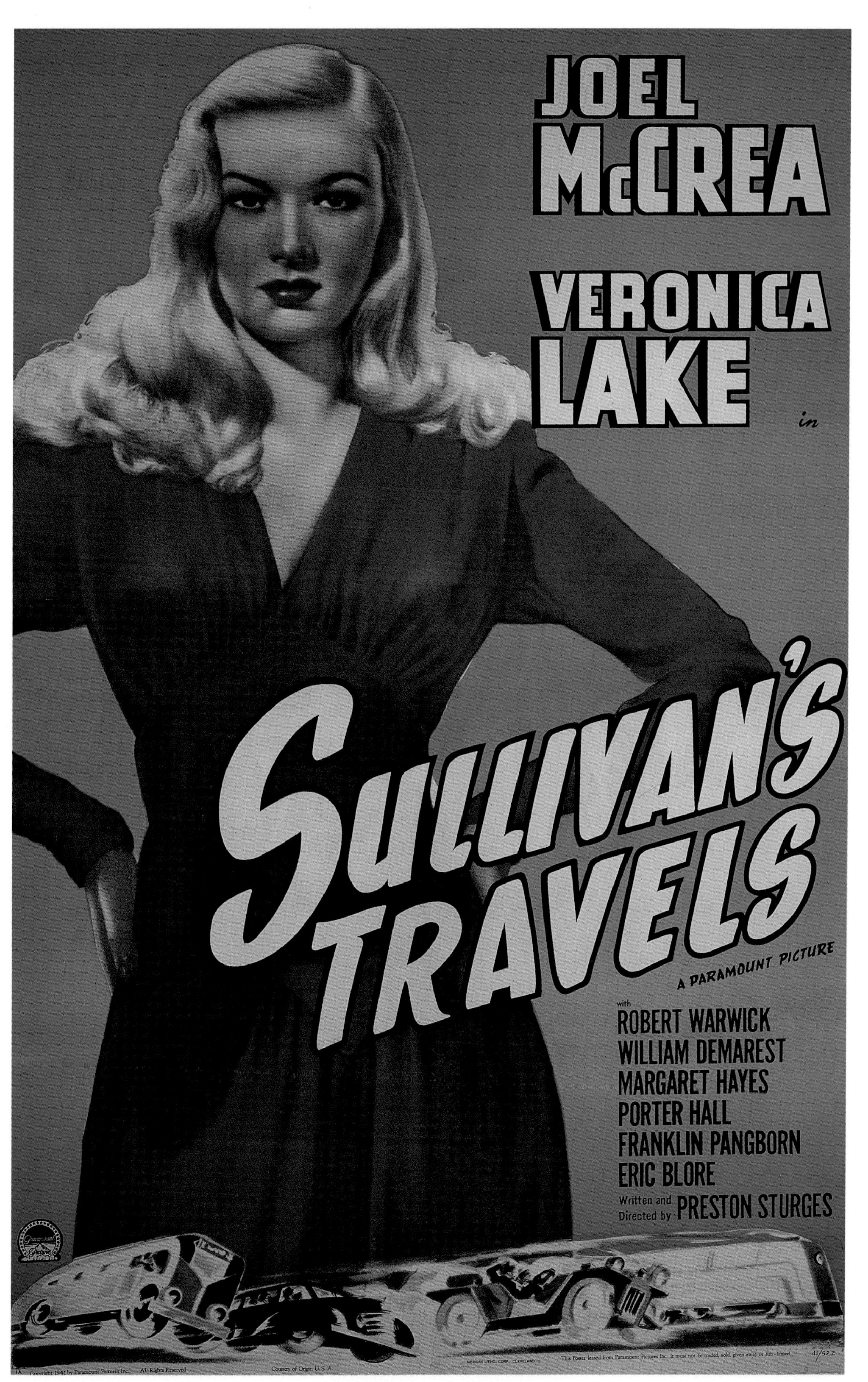

126. SULLIVAN'S TRAVELS, 1942

127. THE MEANEST MAN IN THE WORLD, 1943

128. THAT NAZTY NUISANCE, 1943, title card

129. ARSENIC AND OID LACE, 1944

130. THE PRINCESS AND THE PIRATE, 1944

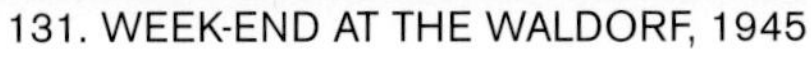

131. WEEK-END AT THE WALDORF, 1945

132. GETTING GERTIE'S GARTER, 1945

133. A NIGHT IN CASABLANCA, 1946

134. ROAD TO UTOPIA, 1946

135. THE KID FROM BROOKLYN, 1946

136. THE FARMER'S DAUGHTER, 1947

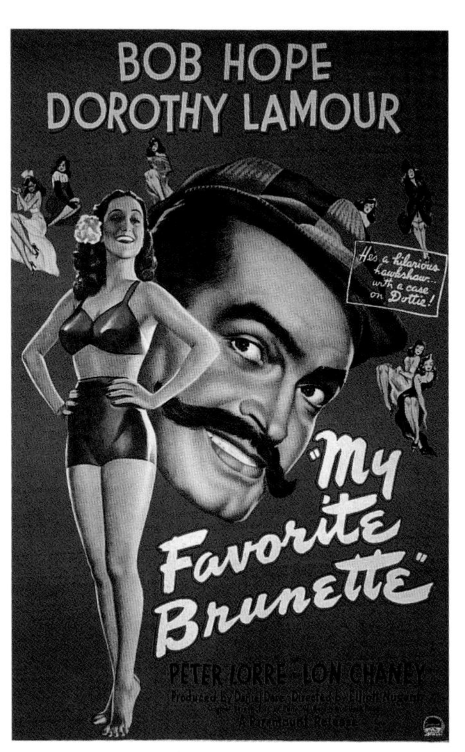

137. MY FAVORITE BRUNETTE, 1947

138. IT'S A JOKE, SON!, 1947

139. SUDDENLY IT'S SPRING, 1947

140. THE SECRET LIFE OF WALTER MITTY, 1947

141. MR. PEABODY AND THE MERMAID, 1948

142. ABBOTT AND COSTELLO MEET FRANKENSTEIN, 1948, lobby card

143. MR. BLANDINGS BUILDS HIS DREAM HOUSE, 1948, lobby card

144. SITTING PRETTY, 1948

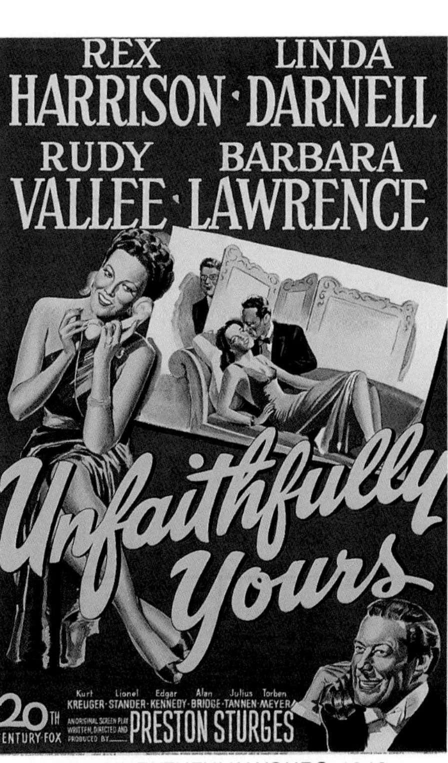

145. UNFAITHFULLY YOURS, 1948

146. THE PALEFACE, 1948

147. THE BEAUTIFUL BLONDE FROM BASHFUL BEND, 1949

148. ABBOTT AND COSTELLO MEET THE KILLER, BORIS KARLOFF, 1949

149. HOLIDAY AFFAIR, 1949

150. ADAM'S RIB, 1949

151. MA AND PA KETTLE, 1949

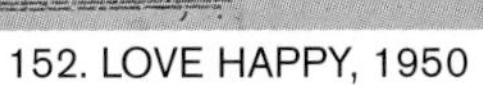
152. LOVE HAPPY, 1950

153. FATHER OF THE BRIDE, 1950

154. THE MILKMAN, 1950

155. THE FULLER BRUSH GIRL, 1950

156. CHEAPER BY THE DOZEN, 1950

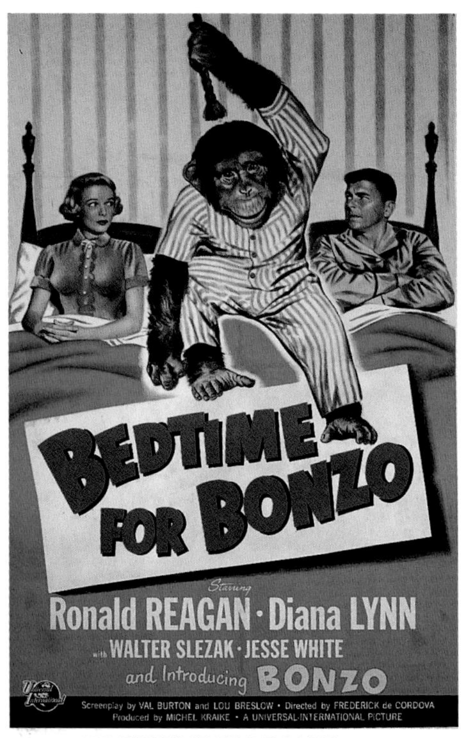

157. BEDTIME FOR BONZO, 1951

158. ABBOTT AND COSTELLO MEET THE INVISIBLE MAN, 1951

159. SON OF PALEFACE, 1952

160. THE LAVENDER HILL MOB, 1951, British one-sheet

161. THE MAN IN THE WHITE SUIT, 1951, British one-sheet

162. SCARED STIFF, 1953, British quad

163. TOP BANANA, 1953, title card

164. GENTLEMEN PREFER BLONDES, 1953

165. THE CADDY, 1953

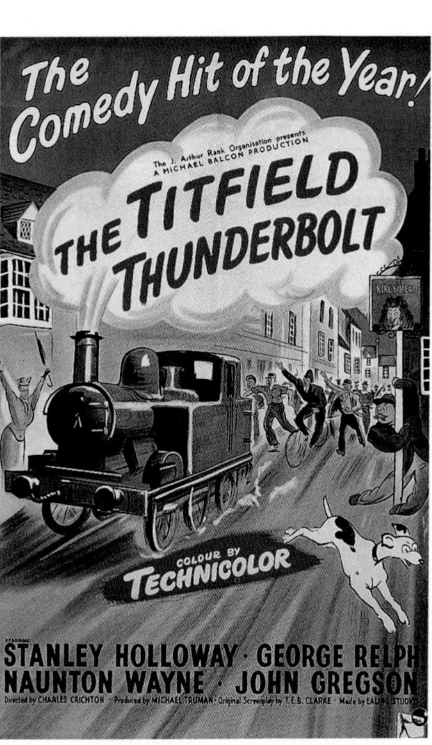

166. THE TITFIELD THUNDERBOLT, 1953, English one-sheet

167. THE LONG, LONG TRAILER, 1954

168. THE SEVEN YEAR ITCH, 1955, French poster

169. DESIGNING WOMAN, 1957

170. THE LADYKILLERS, 1955, British quad

171. DON'T GO NEAR THE WATER, 1957

PARAMOUNT Presents

DANNY KAYE

THE COURT JESTER

COLOR BY TECHNICOLOR

Co-starring

GLYNIS JOHNS

BASIL RATHBONE

ANGELA LANSBURY

CECIL PARKER

Words and Music by
Sylvia Fine and Sammy Cahn

Written, Produced and Directed by
Norman Panama and Melvin Frank

VISTAVISION
MOTION PICTURE HIGH FIDELITY

8005

55 \ 379

172. THE COURT JESTER, 1956

173. SOME LIKE IT HOT, 1959, title card

174. PILLOW TALK, 1959

175. OPERATION PETTICOAT, 1959

176. DARBY O'GILL AND THE LITTLE PEOPLE, 1959

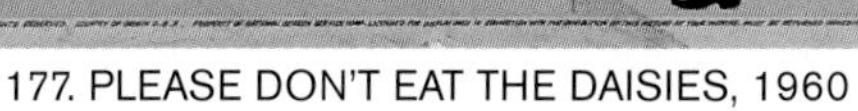
177. PLEASE DON'T EAT THE DAISIES, 1960

178. THE PARENT TRAP!, 1961

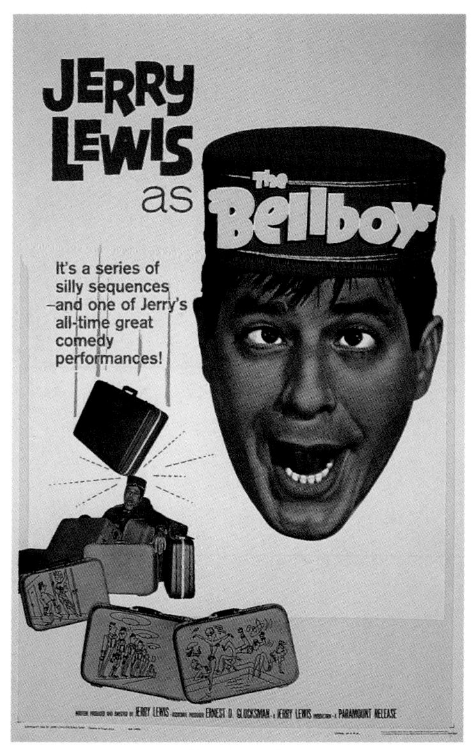

179. THE BELLBOY, 1960

180. THE HONEYMOON MACHINE, 1961

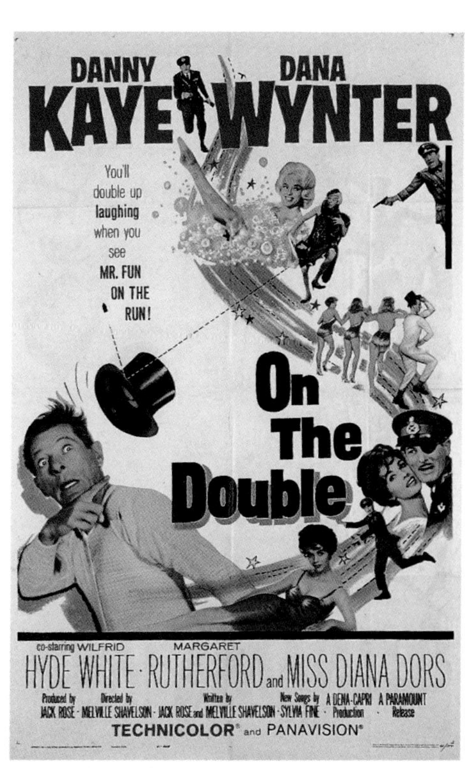

181. ON THE DOUBLE, 1961

182. THAT TOUCH OF MINK, 1962

183. MY GEISHA, 1962

184. MR. HOBBS TAKES A VACATION, 1962

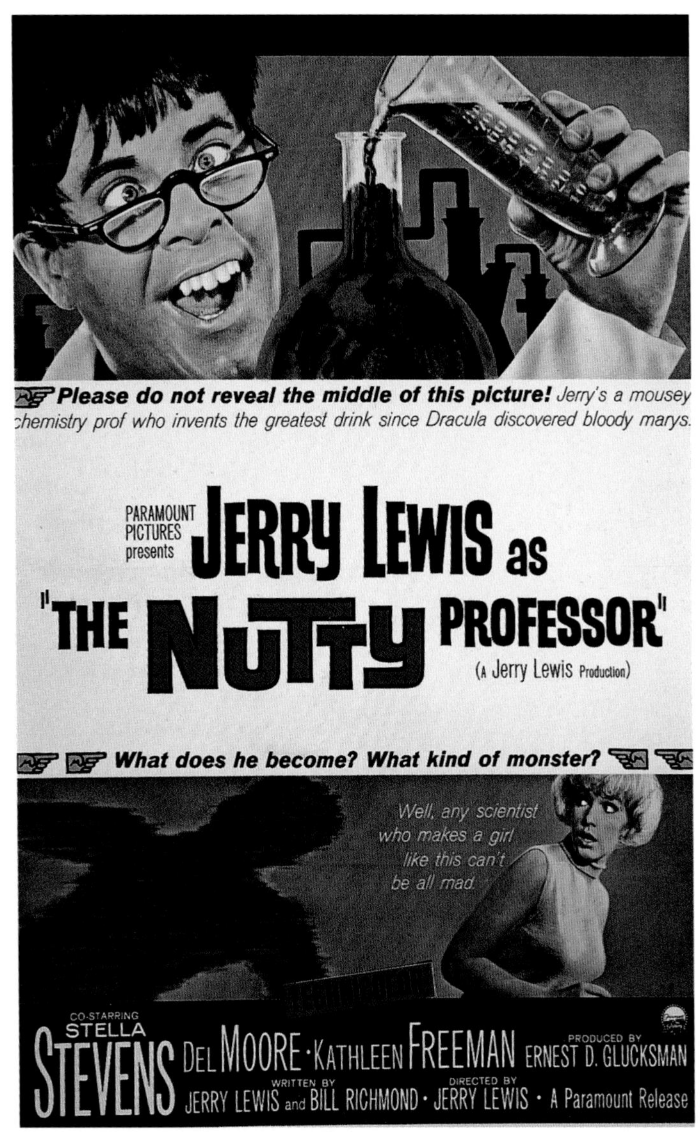

185. THE NUTTY PROFESSOR, 1963

186. IT'S A MAD, MAD, MAD, MAD WORLD, 1963

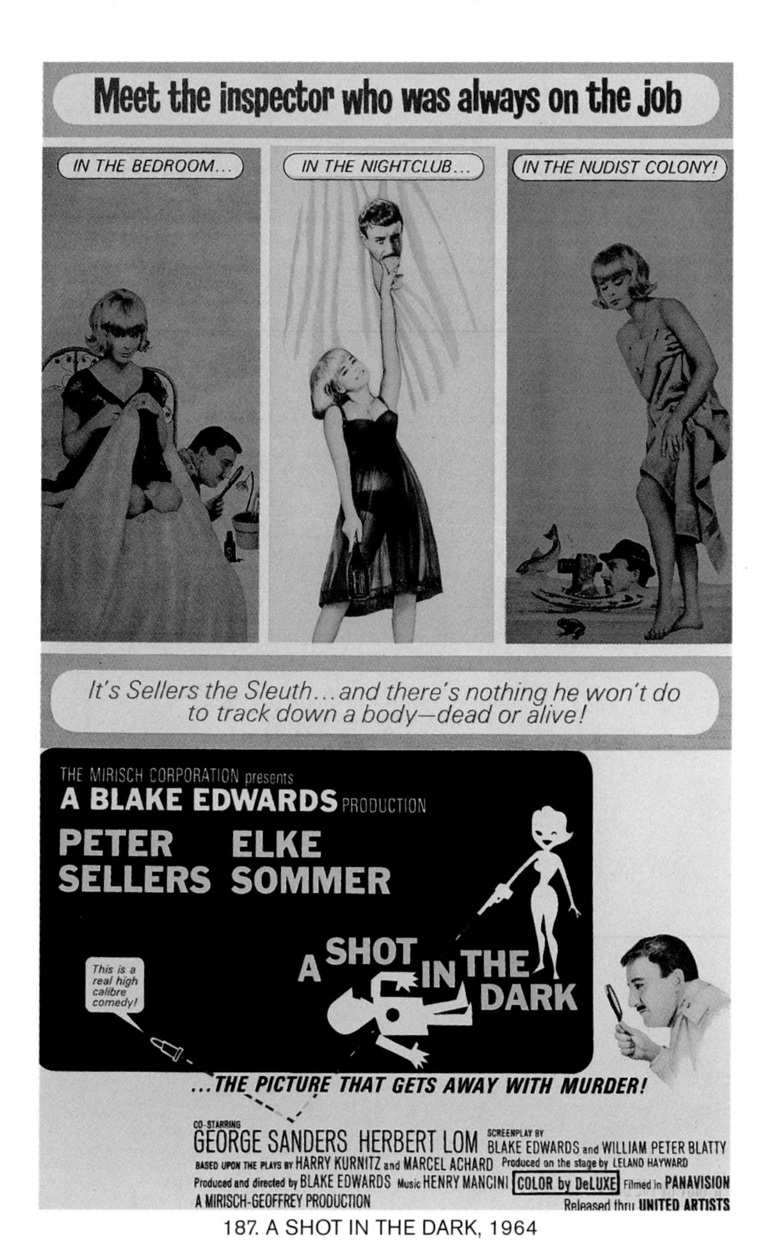

187. A SHOT IN THE DARK, 1964

188. WHAT'S NEW PUSSYCAT?, 1965

189. WHAT A WAY TO GO!, 1964

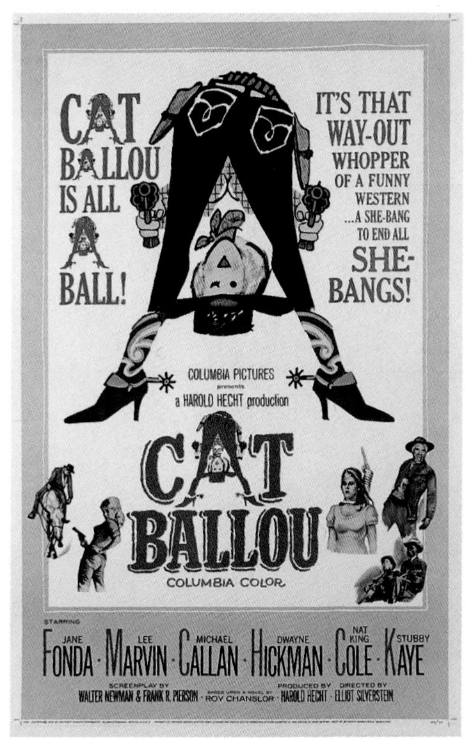

190. CAT BALLOU, 1965

191. THE LOVED ONE, 1965

192. A FUNNY THING HAPPENED ON THE WAY TO THE FORUM, 1966

193. THE FORTUNE COOKIE, 1966

194. THE RUSSIANS ARE COMING, THE RUSSIANS ARE COMING, 1966

195. THE GRADUATE, 1967

196. BEDAZZLED, 1967

197. THE PRODUCERS, 1968

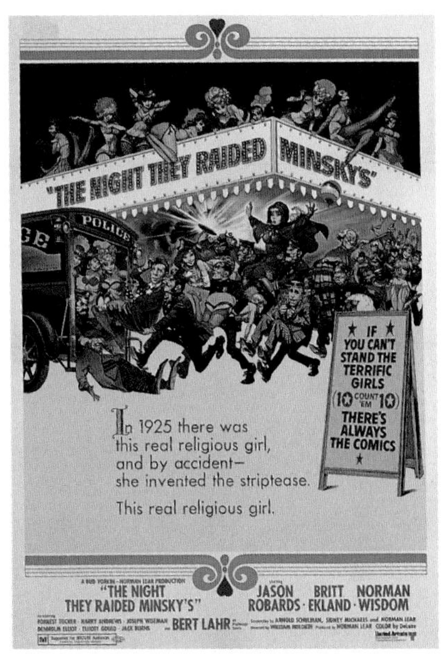

198. THE NIGHT THEY RAIDED MINSKY'S, 1968

199. WHERE WERE YOU WHEN THE LIGHTS WENT OUT?, 1968

200. PRUDENCE AND THE PILL, 1968

201. THE ODD COUPLE, 1968, three-sheet

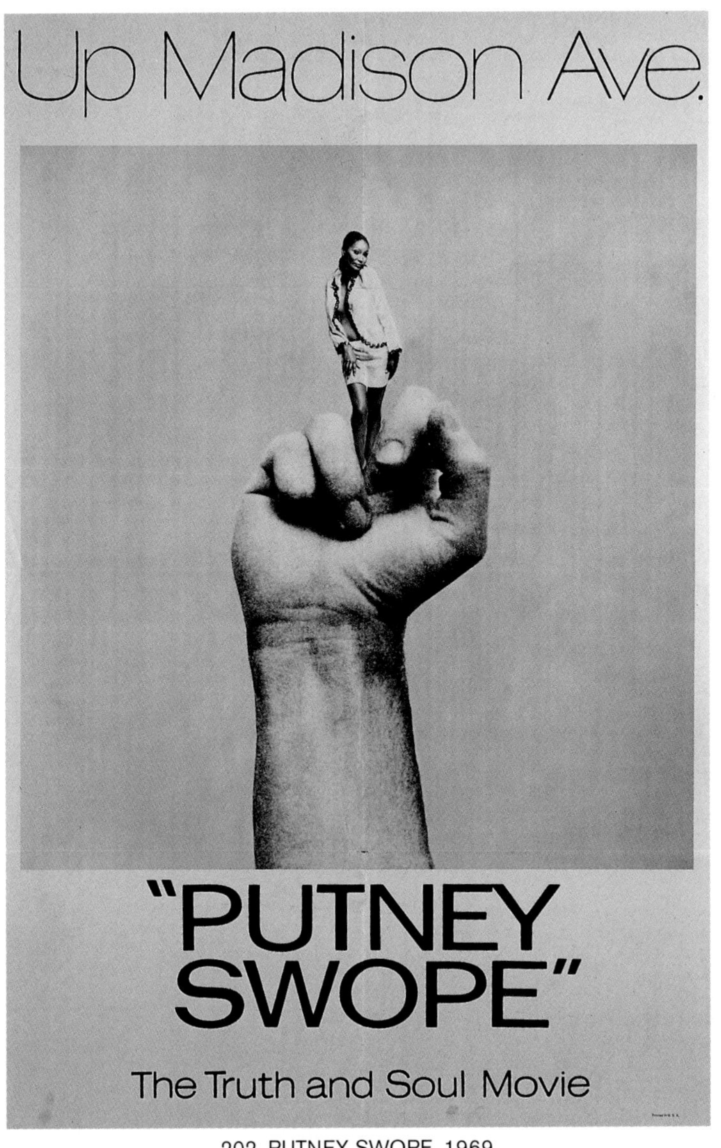

202. PUTNEY SWOPE, 1969

203. THE OUT-OF-TOWNERS, 1970

204. THE LOVE BUG, 1969

205. BOB & CAROL & TED & ALICE, 1969

206. CACTUS FLOWER, 1969

207. BANANAS, 1971

208. COLD TURKEY, 1971

209. WHAT'S UP, DOC?, 1972

210. PLAY IT AGAIN, SAM, 1972

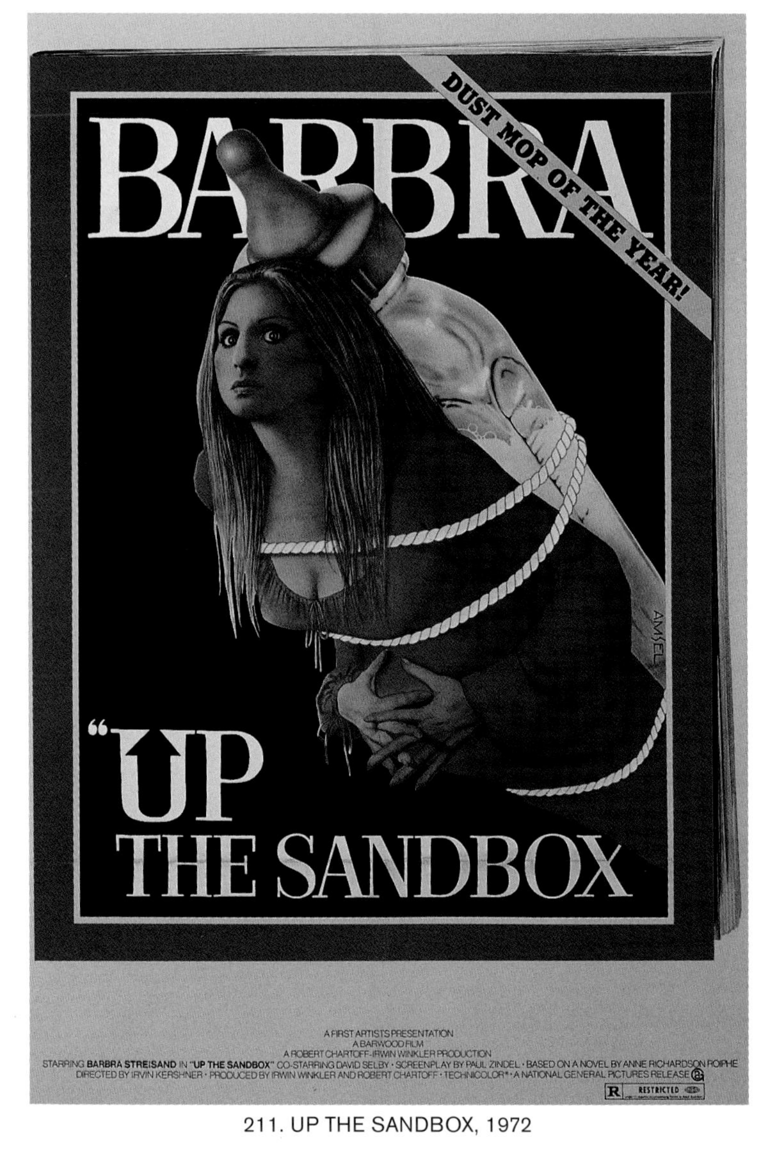

211. UP THE SANDBOX, 1972

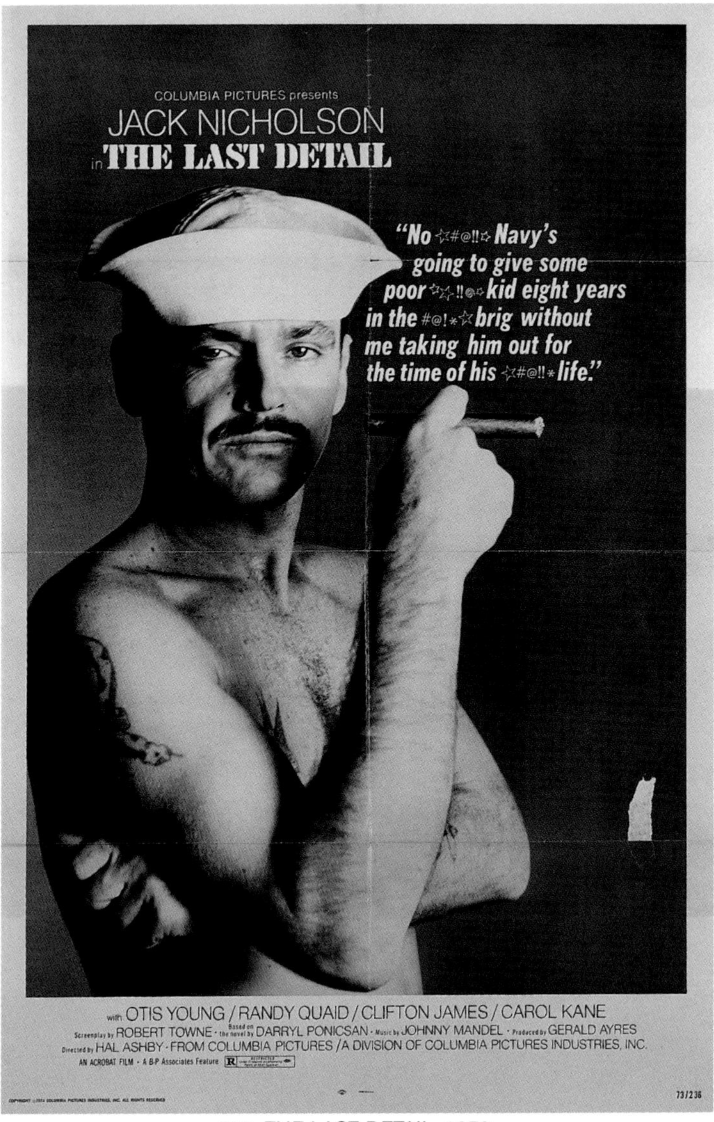

212. THE LAST DETAIL, 1973

213. AMERICAN GRAFFITI, 1973

214. A TOUCH OF CLASS, 1973

215. SLEEPER, 1973

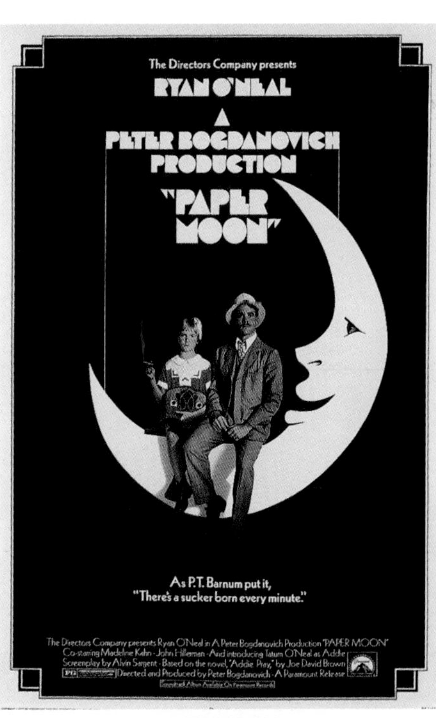

216. PAPER MOON, 1973

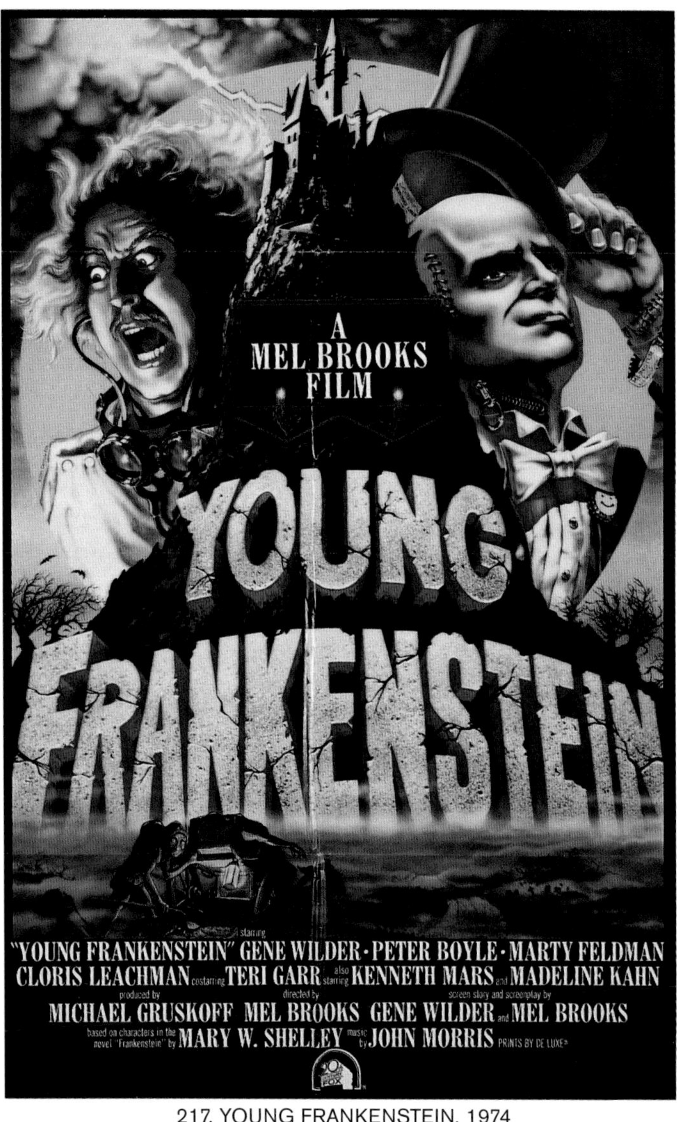

217. YOUNG FRANKENSTEIN, 1974

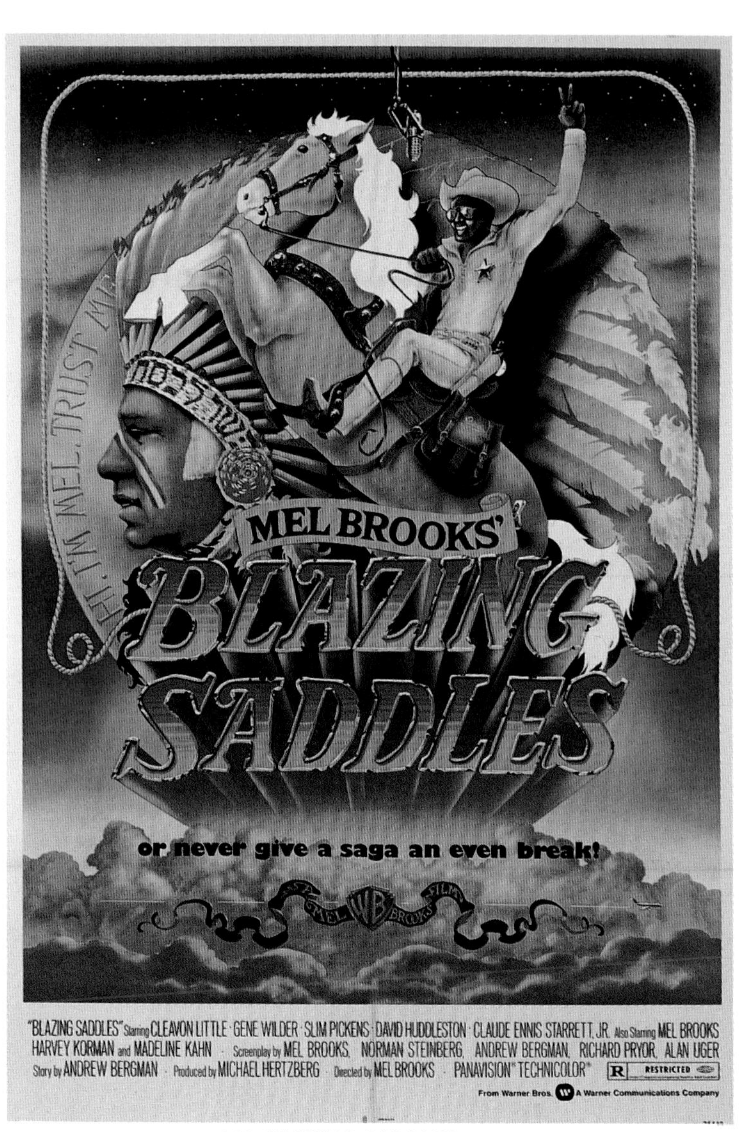

218. BLAZING SADDLES, 1974

219. MONTY PYTHON AND THE HOLY GRAIL, 1975

220. THE SUNSHINE BOYS, 1975

221. LOVE AND DEATH, 1975

222. CAR WASH, 1976

223. KENTUCKY FRIED MOVIE, 1977

224. OH, GOD!, 1977

225. THE BAD NEWS BEARS, 1976

226. SLAP SHOT, 1977

227. NATIONAL LAMPOON'S ANIMAL HOUSE, 1978, subway poster

228. THE END, 1978

229. HOT LEAD AND COLD FEET, 1978

230. RABBIT TEST, 1978

231. EVERY WHICH WAY BUT LOOSE, 1978

232. UP IN SMOKE, 1978

233. LA CAGE AUX FOLLES, 1978

234. BEING THERE, 1979

235. MANHATTAN, 1979

236. THE IN-LAWS, 1979

237. MEATBALLS, 1979

238. MONTY PYTHON'S LIFE OF BRIAN, 1979

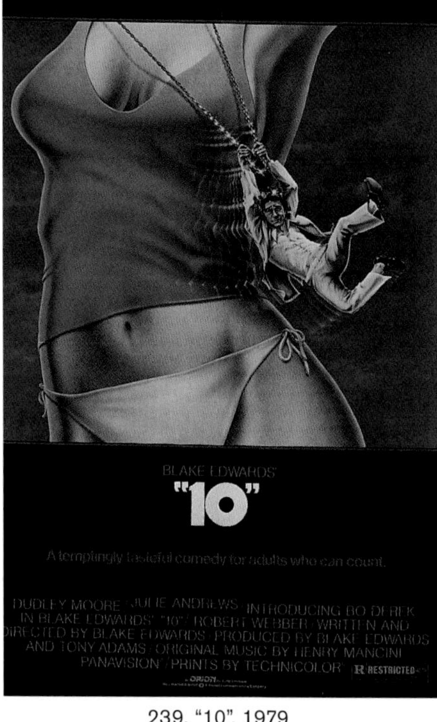

239. "10", 1979

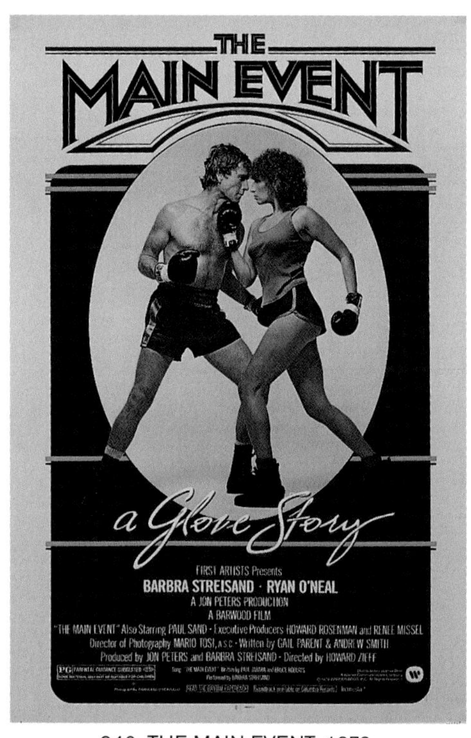

240. THE MAIN EVENT, 1979

241. THE JERK, 1979

242. USED CARS, 1980

243. ANY WHICH WAY YOU CAN, 1980

244. MELVIN (AND HOWARD), 1980

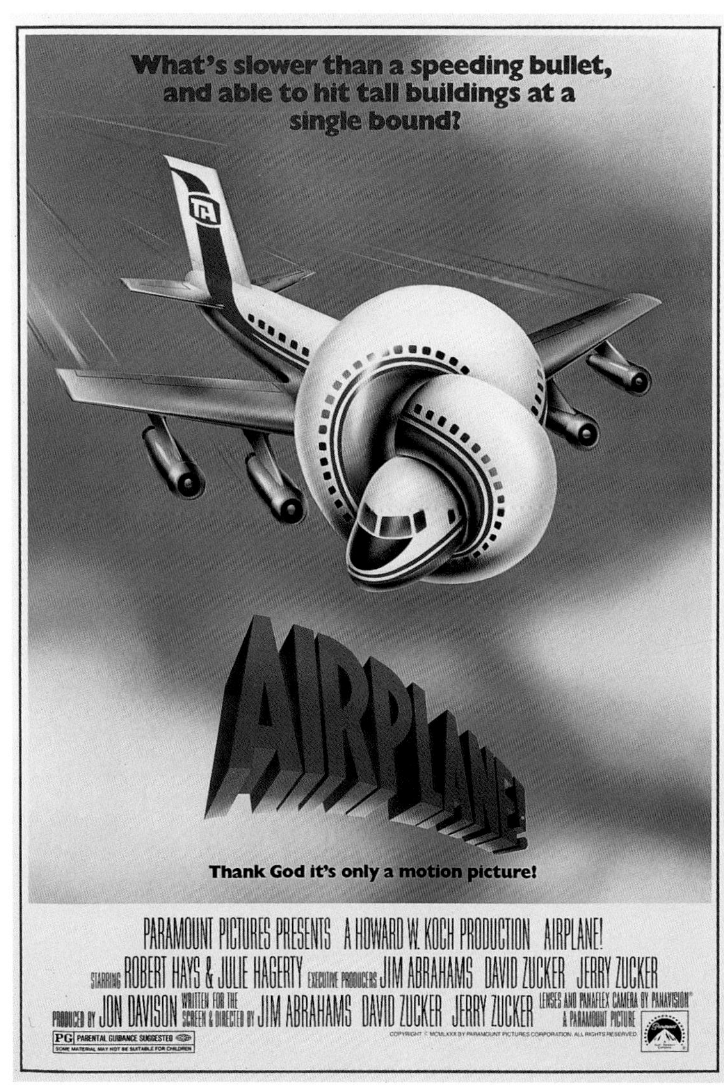

245. AIRPLANE!, 1980

246. STIR CRAZY, 1980

247. NEIGHBORS, 1981

248. ARTHUR, 1981

249. PORKY'S, 1981

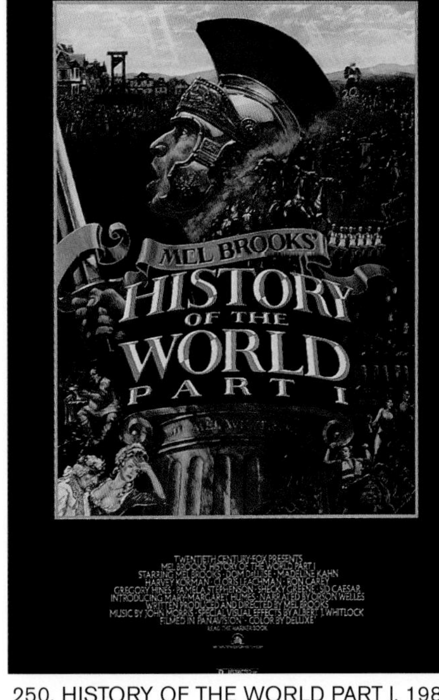

250. HISTORY OF THE WORLD PART I, 1981

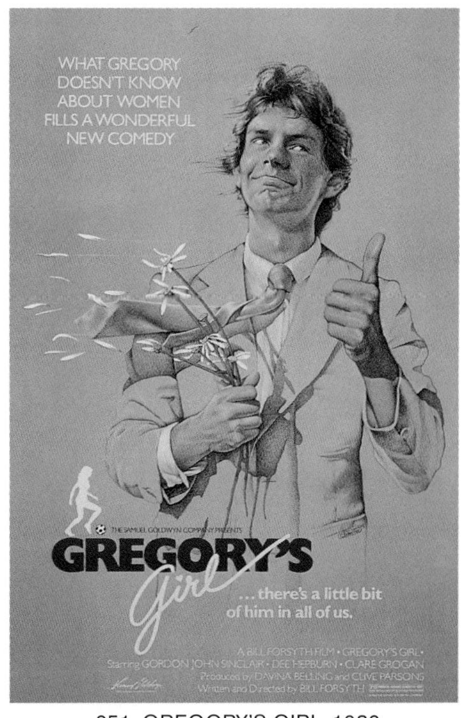

251. GREGORY'S GIRL, 1982

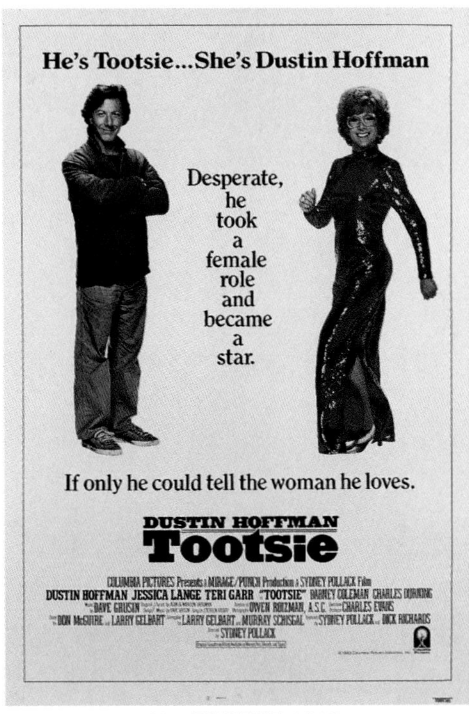

252. TOOTSIE, 1982

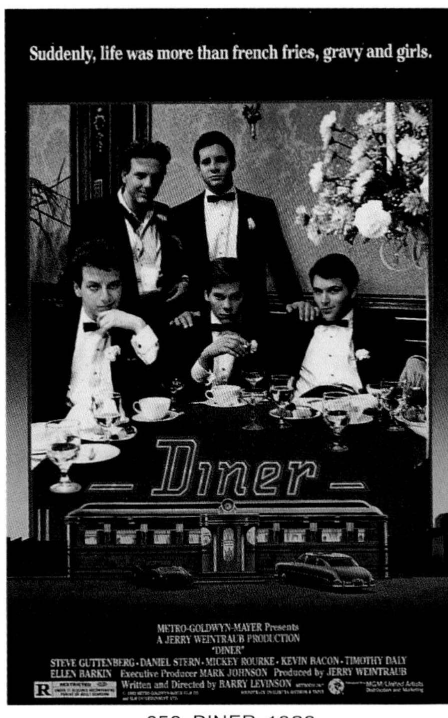

253. DINER, 1982

254. VALLEY GIRL, 1983

255. A CHRISTMAS STORY, 1983

256. MONTY PYTHON'S THE MEANING OF LIFE, 1983

257. SPLASH, 1984

258. BEVERLY HILLS COP, 1984

259. THIS IS SPINAL TAP, 1984

260. BLAME IT ON RIO, 1984

261. THE WOMAN IN RED, 1984

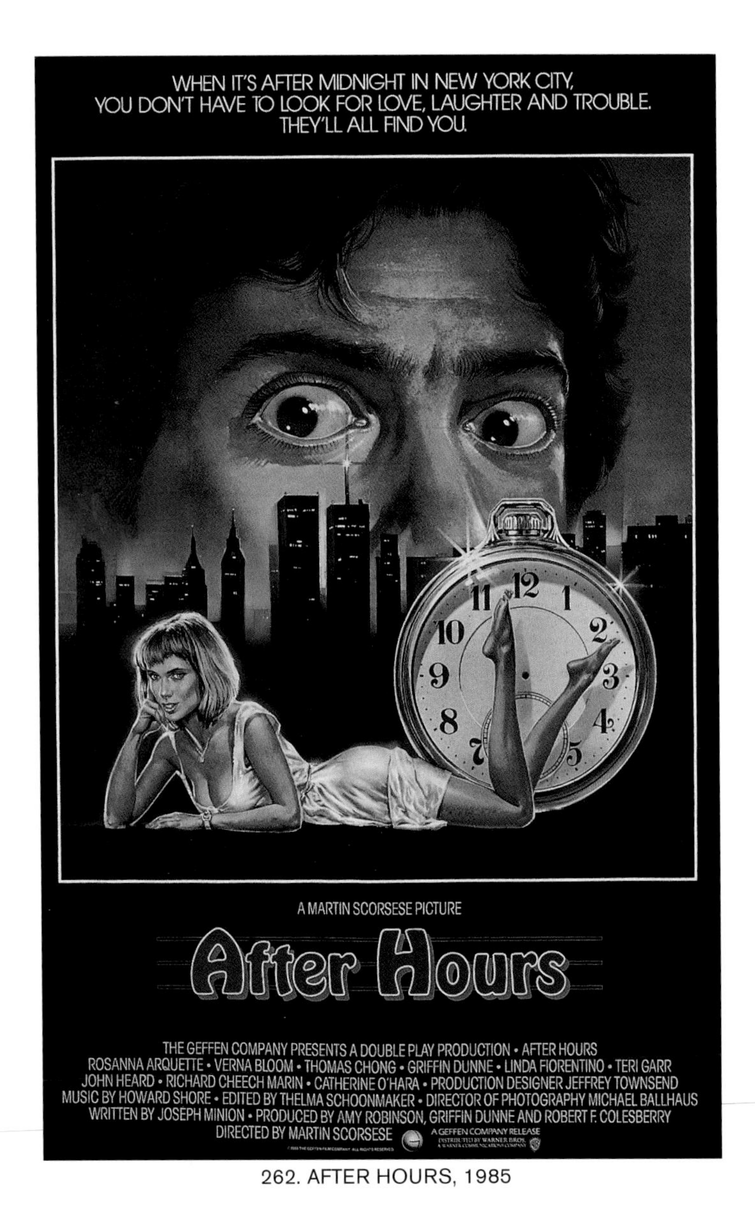

262. AFTER HOURS, 1985

263. "CROCODILE" DUNDEE, 1986

264. NATIONAL LAMPOON'S EUROPEAN VACATION, 1985

265. THREE MEN AND A BABY, 1987

266. RAISING ARIZONA, 1987

267. PLANES, TRAINS AND AUTOMOBILES, 1987

268. A FISH CALLED WANDA, 1988

269. TWINS, 1988

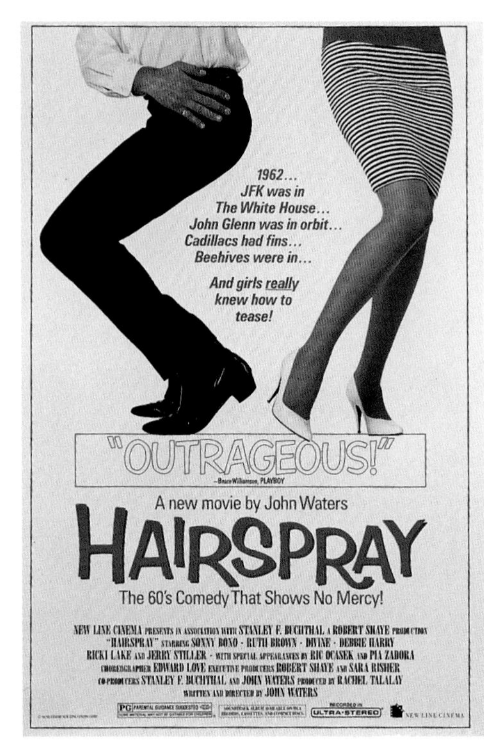

270. HAIRSPRAY, 1988

271. BIG, 1988

272. CINEMA PARADISO, 1988

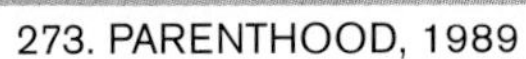

273. PARENTHOOD, 1989

274. WHEN HARRY MET SALLY..., 1989

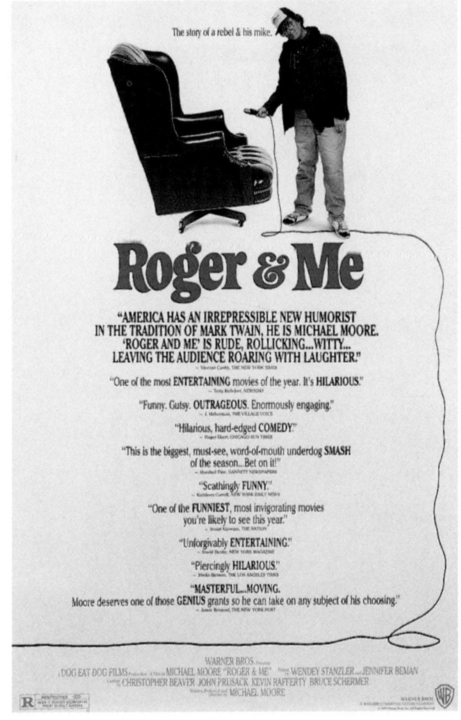

275. ROGER & ME, 1989

276. HARLEM NIGHTS, 1989

277. UNCLE BUCK, 1989

278. PRETTY WOMAN, 1990

279. THE ADDAMS FAMILY, 1991

280. SOAPDISH, 1991

281. HOME ALONE, 1990

282. CITY SLICKERS, 1991

283. HONEYMOON IN VEGAS, 1992

284. MY COUSIN VINNY, 1992

285. THE WEDDING BANQUET, 1993

286. SLEEPLESS IN SEATTLE, 1993

287. MRS. DOUBTFIRE, 1993

288. EAT DRINK MAN WOMAN, 1994

289. FOUR WEDDINGS AND A FUNERAL, 1994

290. IT COULD HAPPEN TO YOU, 1994

291. THE FLINTSTONES, 1994

292. ACE VENTURA WHEN NATURE CALLS, 1995, video poster

293. ACE VENTURA PET DETECTIVE, 1995

294. WHILE YOU WERE SLEEPING, 1995

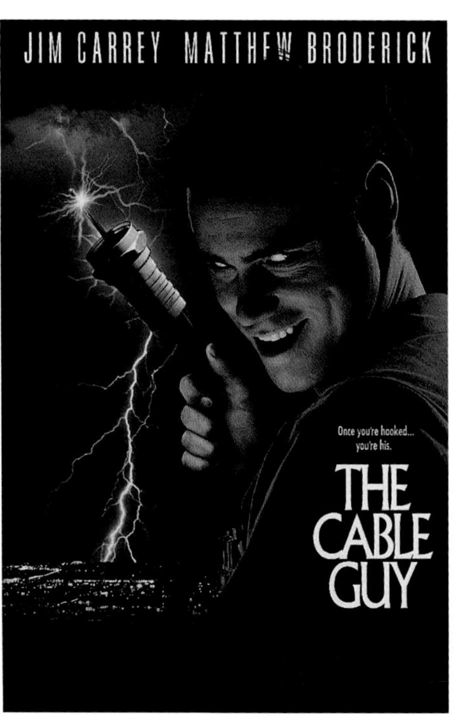

295. THE CABLE GUY, 1996

296. HAPPY GILMORE, 1996

297. CLUELESS, 1995

298. THE NUTTY PROFESSOR, 1996

299. AS GOOD AS IT GETS, 1997

300. MY BEST FRIEND'S WEDDING, 1997

301. FLUBBER, 1997

302. IN & OUT, 1997

303. GEORGE OF THE JUNGLE, 1997

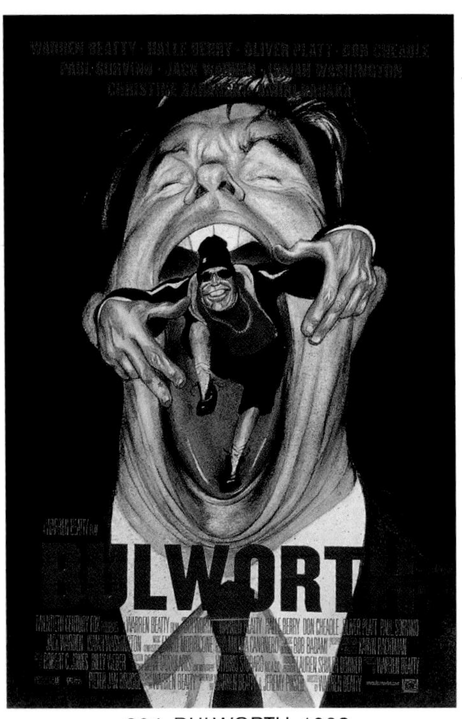

304. BULWORTH, 1998

305. PATCH ADAMS, 1998

306. CELEBRITY, 1998

307. THE TRUMAN SHOW, 1998

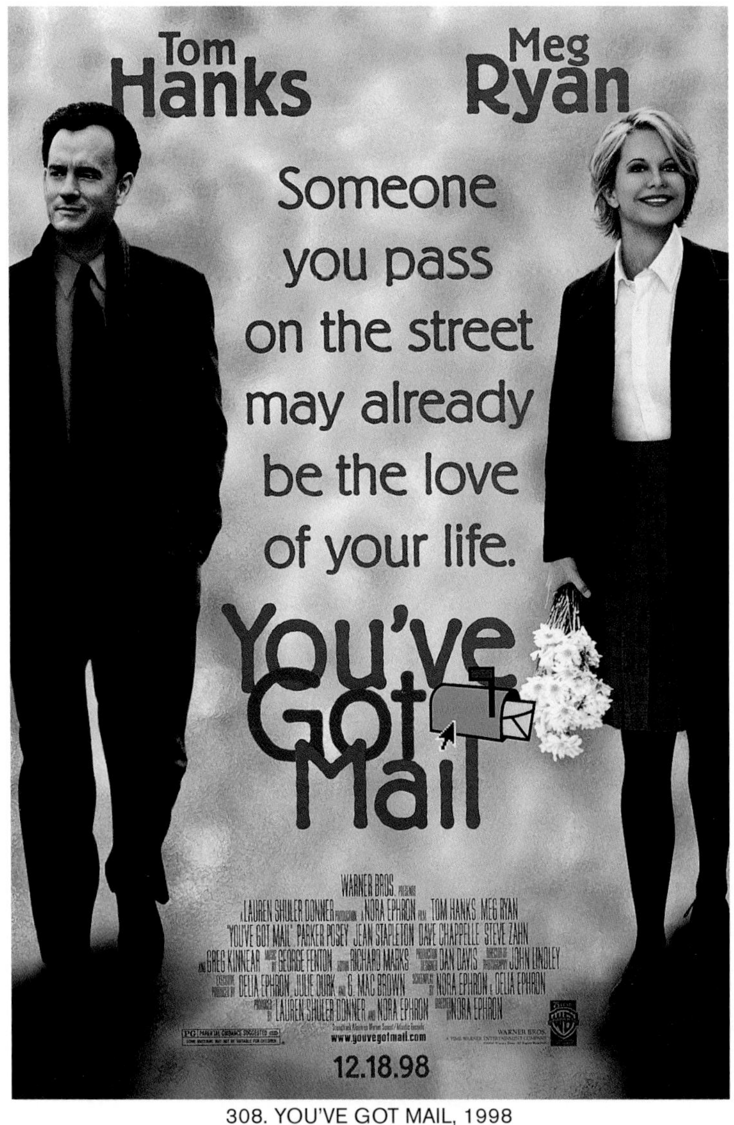

308. YOU'VE GOT MAIL, 1998

309. BIG DADDY, 1999

310. AUSTIN POWERS THE SPY WHO SHAGGED ME, 1999

311. BOWFINGER, 1999

312. ANALYZE THIS, 1999

313. RUNAWAY BRIDE, 1999

314. ME, MYSELF & IRENE, 2000

SHE'S POULTRY IN MOTION

CHICKEN RUN

JUNE 23

Aardman

www.reel.com/chickenrun

DREAMWORKS PICTURES

315. CHICKEN RUN, 2000

316. SMALL TIME CROOKS, 2000

317. 102 DALMATIONS, 2000

318. THE GRINCH, 2000

COMEDY MOVIE POSTERS INDEX

COMEDY MOVIE POSTERS INDEX